INSIDE THE SMILE

TAMSIN HOPKINS

INDEPENDENT INNOVATIVE INTERNATIONAL

Published by Cinnamon Press
Meirion House,
Glan yr afon,
Tanygrisiau
Blaenau Ffestiniog,
Gwynedd, LL41 3SU
www.cinnamonpress.com

The right of Tamsin Hopkins to be identified as author of this work has been asserted by her in accordance with the Copyright, Designs and Patent Act, 1988. Copyright © 2017 Tamsin Hopkins.
ISBN: 978-1-910836-72-9

British Library Cataloguing in Publication Data. A CIP record for this book can be obtained from the British Library.

Designed and typeset in Palatino by Cinnamon Press.
Cover design by Jan Fortune.
Printed in Poland
Cinnamon Press is represented in the UK by Inpress Ltd and in Wales by the Welsh Books Council

Acknowledgements

Some of these poems first appeared in *Envoi, Lampeter Review, Neon Literary Magazine* and *Trio*.

I would like to thank Jan Fortune, Stephen Powell, Kirsty Bradley-Law, Diana Grange Taylor and the many friends and family members who have been so generous with their enthusiasm and patience.

Contents

For
SVHP

Inside the Smile

Nebula Girl is Born

I light a guilty fire
—it's no longer cold,
although April can be chilly.
I don't even empty the grate
but push ash aside
so the fire can breathe.
I make a nest for anthracite
with twigs I've been drying;
as the fire takes, I hear

something

—so I look.

It's getting hot and I can't quite see
—so, hand on chimney breast
one foot in the hearth
I dip my head and squint.
First my hair is drawn
then my forehead, eyes and nose,
then shoulders and the rest has to follow.

I am a film going out of focus
a cartoon girl
Mary Poppins in reverse
no umbrella.

I travel through, like
a worm hole, like
a sooty birth canal
to a new dimension.

Instead of coming out the top
of the chimney pot with a satisfying pop
I am atoms, girl ash
dispersing particles each with an eye
that looks down on my house. I float
towards the interstellar spaces I will fill.

I am a new nebula.

The Rissos and the boy

They're not the pretty ones—
but they're the ones that wait for him.

Long pale shadows
against the black sea.
Scarred from fights,
neckless, shrewd-eyed
they swim on their backs
to see him—dark against the sky.
Undulating, revolving slowly,
they see how he swims
keeping up for meters.
The leader watching
matches his pace
and they slow, turn over,
flip languid tails for a while,
and he is a long pale shadow
undulating with them.

Then, with a flick

one quick look
they are away
into black clouds of deep Atlantic
and he—is a boy in the sea again.

Three Dreams about Birds' Feet

Birds' Feet

I wake up in the bath with them under me and all over me, scaly and scratchy, they have little red ringlets inside yellow skin and sucked like a vacuum, sucked around a white core of bone stick and they scratch me everywhere. I have to push myself into them to get out of the bath; they bend like spiky yellow and red ink, they twirl, they flow down the plughole. I look in the mirror and nothing's wrong so I get into bed without drying myself and wake up in the bath, full of bird's feet.

Albatross

A glider. An albatross. Effortless, majestic, equally unconcerned. The pilot wants to see what the albatross sees but her cowardice, her avarice, get in the way. Her big black fly-eye sunglasses do not protect, so she sees only glinting sunlight squiggling off the waves, semaphore, or Morse that she knows and understands, but can't signal back.
She can't land, because the glider has no feet.

Reflection on the swan

I am the reflection of a swan, gliding on a glass lake; my head is carried straight down but I am looking up, down to my feet.
My feet are clasped with the swan's feet, rotating and pedalling under the water to keep it looking smooth but I bob deeper, up and down each time he paddles. He is not aware of me, I am a shadow attached to him by the feet. I can cock my head majestically, keep a calm eye, but the feet, oh the feet are a mess and give it all away.
Also, I am drowning. But you can't tell this to the swan.

Also, I am drowning. But you can't tell this to the swan.

Also, I am drowning. But you can't tell this to the swan.

Diving Free

We were there for a week.
The water was cold, the beach stony,
volcanic and thin, falling away to nothing.

I swam every day in the morning
again in the evening.
I used the same yellow towel.

'Aren't you coming in?' I asked
and later every day I said
'It's warmer now' so she would know.

There were no fish.
I could see the rocks a long way down
black under my shadow.

I practised holding my breath
meditated
performed sun salutations on the balcony.

'Freedivers achieve up to 75%
greater lung capacity with practice
and stretches,' I told her.

Her mind was on other things.
She said she could, she would,
but I never saw her swim.

I didn't have time to improve.
I swam deep and far, pumped up my heart
as best I could.

When I knew she couldn't see me
I lay on my back and waited.
Alone, I still hoped for stars.

Terracotta Stairway

My son holds a photo:
Who is this woman?

I look. I am surprised.
Her clothes are natural
I still like her taste.
She is tanned, healthy,
dark hair to the waist
she is perhaps beautiful
bright with love.

It was in Tuscany, I say
taken by a stranger.
I forget the day.

There were herbs tumbling
crowding red masonry
pressing through footworn steps

lavender, oregano, rosemary,
thyme underfoot.

I trailed my hand through silver stems
stole a lavender head,

and oh, the smell
              when I crushed it.

Truncated Venus

They said it was a mercy,
a blessing, long overdue.
The tree is dying.
Is dangerous.
Is dead.

I watch the mechanical cacophony
hour upon surgical hour, hours
of precision, destruction.

I watch.
I stretch out this brittle hand,
remember
blood receding
from drying limbs.

I feel the memory
of truncated stumps,

lost synapses
that whisper to me

of holding fruit
of the softest cheek
of knowing lace
of piano keys
of my own embrace

and like that unresisting tree
I want your hope
your cleansing cut
and if I pay you enough

will you do it to me now?
will you do it to me quickly?

Expectorate

Up it came, undeniable,
from the deep unfelt .

First the gurgle,
the emphysema glottal stop
awash in her throat.

Then it was hack, hack, hack,
she thought the coughing cracked her skull,
that a fragment would drop into her hand.

Next the glurping began;
from lower down, a pumping peristalsis
that produced
nothing.

Then, lower still
a stirring deep below:

a pause, a glance,
up it came in a rush
    —a wet pebble, perfectly heavy.

A dead egg.

So, it was true what he had said—
deep down, deep inside,
she was made of stone.

Cold Ariadne and the Wolf in my Head

tumtum tumtum   tumtum tumtum   tumtum tumtum

We run, the wolf and I,
night after night—
his strides spin the world

Hah   hah   hah   hah   hah   hah
  thump   thump   thump   thump   thump
    thump   thump   thump   thump   thump

hot breath orders my blood,
the tundra thump of his feet
summon her spirit.

Hah   hah   hah   hah   hah   hah   hah   hah   hah   hah

   thump
    thump
      thump
       thump
         thump
          thump
            thump
             thump
               thump
                thump

With that double drum
he builds his spell – soon
she must reveal herself.

Hah   hah   hah   hah   hah   hah
  thump   thump   thump   thump   thump
    thump   thump   thump   thump   thump

Together, the white wolf and I,
we *will* find my sister.

tumtum **tumtum**   **tumtum** **tumtum**   **tumtum** **tumtum**

Hah   hah   hah   hah   hah   hah   hah   hah   hah   hah

thump
   thump
      thump
         thump
            thump
               thump
                  thump
                     thump
                        thump
                           thump

Hah   hah   hah   hah   hah   hah
thump   thump   thump   thump   thump
   thump   thump   thump   thump   thump

tumtum **tumtum**   **tumtum** **tumtum**   **tumtum** **tumtum**

17

Cuttlefish Kiss

Eye to eye
she accepted the claustrophobia
of his embrace, the cold flesh pressed
into her chest and face, the questing tendrils,
firm yet delicate.

Luminous ligatures held her chin,
began their curlicue exploration
via the throat,
found her liver
caressed her spleen
gently touched each vertebra
on the inside.

In a rush of rising pulp,
a tourniquet of insistent flesh
filled her spinal column
forced open her cerebellum
penetrated temporal lobes
pushing on through bone and scalp
until living extrusions emerged
like questing elvers,
squirming, vermicular—
a many-eyed
wig.

Death by Kissing

All of us girls arrive together and stick together and laugh too loud and look over their shoulders, have they seen me, has he seen me, who has come with that one and this one and what's he wearing and is he going to dance?

And I didn't get the one I liked and nor did he, so we thought we might as well, so we locked lips, joined hips and stayed like that all night and we both decided it would be more of a success if we had love bites to show, so he sucked my neck and I've got two moles there now which look like teeth marks which is what it felt like and I sucked his neck; it was greasy.

*

Somewhere in all those years, all that passion, that roiling and boiling and doing it when you're not supposed to, where you're not supposed to, somebody, and I'm fairly sure who, *and* when, gave me a dose of herpes vulgaris, thankfully only on the mouth, which comes and goes but has meant at times I have been unable to kiss my husband or my children, careful not to brush the baby's head with contaminated lips or to share a spoon or cup or glass, isolating my cutlery—because I love them.

*

And now I lie down, waiting, and he rolls on top of me and does his washing machine routine with his tongue and I don't know where his mind is—but it isn't with me and I drop my tongue to the back of my throat, retreat, so my mouth is dry like a cave and I try to notice if he's noticed, but his eyes are closed and his machine is still churning and then he says good night and turns out his light, and I swallow my love with his saliva.

Silver Incision

She had made pudding—cherry pie, his favourite.
He smiled, shrugged his cuff, said he didn't have time.
He wasn't sure what he wanted. She tutted. She knew.
He wanted to go *and* he didn't want
anyone else to have his slice.

He looked at her bone white china,
took up the tiny teaspoon and synapse quick,
cut out, flipped up a sugary lid,
removed one surgical cherry,
glistening red and whole.

He moved his espresso cup and placed the small orb
centred smack in the coffee areola.
He smiled, kissed her
and left.

Half a New Life

He turned up
at the annual company do
with a sweet young thing
who made him smile
and look like the man
he might have been
—before he met
the unhappy one
who I presume
has kept the children

Headache—mostly grey

I sit in the grey and wait
for my headache to leave.

Through eyelashes I look where the window should be,
white bars where the material doesn't meet.

Later—I mumble on dry toast that has too much butter on it
or not enough butter on it,
it catches in my throat.
If I cough, my eyes will split like a cat, possibly Schrodinger's,
like a cat in space
with eyes going supernova only there will be noise,
brain curdling noise,
simultaneous annihilation by sound and light,

so I don't gag.
I hardly breathe.
I sip warm water
with my eyes shut.
I want a bath
but I can't waste the water of the world
for my body,
so I wait in the grey.

Later—you come in, being what you think is quiet
but which is the quiet of a toddler
investigating a toy cupboard in the dark.
I look at you with my eyelids
and for the first time I think I know what 'aura' means
—people who glow in the dark.
I wouldn't mind keeping that
but not with this much pain,
so I wait, in the grey.

Later—my feet are hot
   and my hands are hot
   my eyes are sweating
   but my back is cold
   so I lie spread out, a scarecrow executed at dusk
   floral rectangle for a body, eyes under a cloth
   seeking grey.

Later—the tablets make me sick
   and the bile toast blocks the sink with its butter
   and the clock ticks are too loud
   and your TV makes me sit up and I can't leave
   but you want to come to bed and make noise
   like fantastic fireworks
   next to me
   in the grey.

Juanita changes her destiny

I will not follow to the mountain
to drink and die and freeze for them.

I will walk
            until I find the dunes
then dig a hollow
            until it falls on me.

I will sleep there, foetal,
my life a libation to the sands.

I will not rot or stink and putrefy,
but will desiccate, a desert sacrifice,

with twisted cheeks, snarling teeth,
tattoos and patchy orange hair

and they will wonder why
            I needed nothing with me
                        in my afterlife.

Rapunzel at JFK

to be read in the voice of Philip Seymour-Hoffman, RiP

The plane was delayed, the passengers corralled
safe against the storm.
She was alone.

Maybe she was going to her lover
but I didn't think so, she was
too comfortable, too self-contained.

A sinuous dance, her hair
fell in one strong braid
swinging lazy, over her shoulder,

she had a round face
good lips, tanned natural hands
all that was charming

and that way of talking to children
—a sticky toddler gave her something yellow
from a precious plastic bag.

She accepted, head to one side,
slipped off her back pack to kneel by him.
She listened.
It was quite a picture.

I thought about her, three rows in front of me.
Girl, your braid is beautiful,
fabulous long, flexible
like a thick silk rope.
It would be alive in my hand.

Perfect girl – you carry your tower with you
but I am thinking here – with one strong pull,
I can bring it down.

Portrait of the Author in a Lemon Grove

after Jennifer Clement

Dark leaves
bright fruits—
memories

from the year I lived in a lemon tree.

No terrace plants
contained, ignored

but deep in the company of strong green trees.

White flowers
fragrant oils
blessed my palms.

Sleep embraced me among those whispering leaves

with citrus cheek
turned to night breeze

I dreamed their sibilant stories.

Night Swim

The ocean closes dark and hard,
a black mirror alive in the moonlight.

I am a fly, or a water boatman
sculling circles above toxic salt.

A silent shearwater angles near me,
a speeding crucifix intent on home.

There is movement beneath me,
surging enormity; there is—shape.

I see nothing, hear nothing, feel only the swell,
endless depth drawing my viscera.

I do not shout—who would hear?

Later, I hear an echo
                    and I do shout.

I Send the Warrior in Me

after Pascale Petit

I

She wears me
like loose pyjamas.

I am a weightless sheath,
she has all the strength.

She makes horse stance
squat and strong
punches fists, twists
withdraws—lightening
that has me snap
at her elbow.

I fear
only the moment when she will undress
and I fall
           formless
                  at her feet.

II

The warrior in me
comes at need.

With a cry she breasts the hill
black hair snapping
with the mane of her stallion.

No beauty
her nose beak sharp
eyes—dark lasers.

She is what I need.

She lights the fire with dry dung
hides our tracks
says little.

Fire doused with coffee grounds
the warrior woman leaps astride her piebald familiar
reaches for my arm
pulls me up behind her.

III

Bone white warrior
mermaid
with trident.

A crystal flash
beam bright
she cuts the shadows.

Her floating hair
frail shoulders
are a lie.

She has killing teeth
inside that smile.

IV

She is a ski racer
for fun.

Her limbs are white fire
her head a bullet.

The mountain calls
she—*is* the answer.

Speed relaxes her.

V

MI5 bitch
corporate witch
human rights lawyer
Sea Shepherd leader
social worker
trauma doctor
healer armed in faith?

Priestess
          Empress
                  Chariot
                        Star